Jude Prunes Trees

By Carmel Reilly

This is Jude.

She loves trees.

She prunes them when they get too big.

Jude has a lot of tools
to do her job.

She has ropes and
a big cutting tool.

Jude is with her friend Drew.

Jude has a rule to keep safe.

Put on a hard hat and boots!

Jude and Drew prune some big trees.

The trees grew too high.

Jude must cut them away from the lines.

Jude's truck has a big tub.

Drew gets into the tub
to reach the high trees.

Jude gets out her cutting tool.

She cuts a few big bits
off a tree.

Drew threw the bits into a chute.

Wood chips come out
the other end!

Then, Jude and Drew trim some little trees.

The trees look like statues!

The next day, they go to a house.

A big wind blew a tree
onto the roof.

Jude gets a rope.

She drags the tree
off the house.

Then Drew chops the tree
into little chunks.

Next, Jude and Drew pull up
a very big tree.

Its roots have dug into the road.

Jude loves her job.

Each day is something new!

CHECKING FOR MEANING

1. How does Drew reach the high trees to trim them? *(Literal)*

2. How are wood chips made? *(Literal)*

3. Why is it important to wear a hard hat when cutting or trimming trees? *(Inferential)*

EXTENDING VOCABULARY

rule	What is a *rule*? When should you follow a rule? Is it sometimes or all the time?
prune	What does it mean to *prune* a tree? What are other words with a similar meaning? E.g. trim, shape, clip, lop, snip, cut.
chute	What shape is a *chute*? Look at this word. What is unusual about the way it is written? Do you know any other words where *ch* makes the /sh/ sound? E.g. machine, chef.

MOVING BEYOND THE TEXT

1. What are some rules you have at home and at school? Why do we have rules?

2. Jude has special tools for her job. Think of another job and the special tools that are needed to do it.

3. If you could make a statue out of a tree, what would you make? A dog? A cat? Why?

4. Talk about why people are told to stay inside when there is a bad storm.

SPEED SOUNDS

oo	ue	ew	ui	u_e

ou	u	oe	o

PRACTICE WORDS

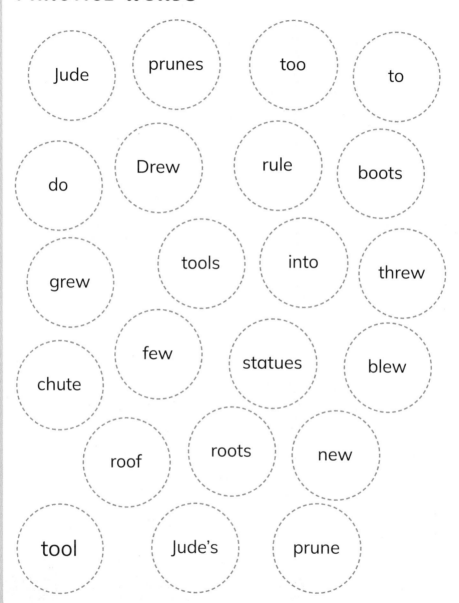

Jude

prunes

too

to

do

Drew

rule

boots

grew

tools

into

threw

few

chute

statues

blew

roof

roots

new

tool

Jude's

prune